Past Life Press

During the Apocalypse

Steffan Piper

Other works by the Author:

Novels:

Yellow Fever
Waiting for Andre
Greyhound
Exit

Poetry Compilations:

Electronic Butterflies
Observations of a Dead Man
During the Apocalypse

ISBN: 9780615145594

During the Apocalypse

DURING THE APOCALYPSE ...

During the Apocalypse
You'll be the dust
Under my boot

Surrounded by waste
Covered in Ash
And running for dear life

During the Apocalypse
You'll be the tears
Running down my cheek
You'll still be the face I see
When I sleep

But you'll probably slow me
Make me linger
Hesitate

You'll probably make me carry you
Share my food with you
Keep you safe

During the Apocalypse
All hell will be on our heels
And there will be
No way back
I'll be screaming for you
To keep up
Reload
Get down

During the Apocalypse
I probably won't be able to save us
But no matter what
I won't leave you

BUREAUCRATIC INERTIA …

If you can't hear the
   Ticking
Then you're just not
   Listening
If you don't feel the
   Black Canvass Bag
    Going slowly over your head
Then you're just not
   Looking
If you don't feel the
   Handcuffs keeping you
    Patiently restrained
Then you're just not
   Cooperating
    Try to pick up a gun
    Try to step out of line
    Try to say something
    That doesn't quite agree
    With their message
If you can't hear the static
Then you're just not
   Paying Attention …

DEEP THOUGHT ...

Shitbird ...
  I've got news for you
You're standing outside
  And you're looking in
    Watching me eat
      Watching me thrive
Unclear about what you're looking at
Unclear about how you feel
Unclear about where
        you
        actually
        stand

Shitbird ...
  I've got news for you
You're outside without a jacket
  And it's raining
    And you're looking at me
      Staring out at you
       In my black pinstripe suit
      warm
      dangerous
      quiet
Unclear about your next move
Unclear about your jealousy
Unclear about your rage
      that's
      burning
      inside you

Shitbird – now listen ...
  I've got news for you
This is important
    Fuck AIDS in Africa ...
    How about AIDS in your bloodstream?
    Fuck Soylent Green and Mad Cow ...
    How about Green Jello and Big Mac's
        -    horse hoofs & hormone beef?

Fuck Acid Rain …
How about Planetary drought?
Fuck the war in the middle east …
How about a Biological Pandemic,
       Germ Warfare or a flesh eating virus?
              You should be concerned,
              But you're not.
              You should be thinking deep, Mate,
              But you're not.

Shitbird …
   You're too busy trying to be
    a better consumer
You're far too concerned about
       Social climbing
       Acquisition of cheap plastic crap
       Struggling to fit in
       All the proper mod-cons
       Playing by the bureaucracy
Just like a real Shitbird
       That's you – the Shitbird

Shitbird …
   I've got news for you
    This is the last thing now -
It's important
       I don't have any answers
       I probably never will
       This isn't poetry
       About your broken heart
       It's not a haiku
       About a one-night-stand
       This isn't some bullshit tale
       About my own petty self-indulgence
       It's not a sermon
       About everything you did that was wrong

Quite the opposite
           It's about all you're about to do
I wouldn't break a sweat though, Shitbird …
You've got some – real – sunny days ahead.

4

YOU NEVER TRAVELED THROUGH TIME …

John Titor
  Screwing with nerds
    Fooling them all, or
      At least you think so …

Did you piss in the coffee
  too many times at the office?
    How disgruntled are you?

You never traveled through time, bro.
You never traveled through time.

The government didn't invest billions, bro
  to have you vacation to 1999
    and posture on the BBS boards
    about low-science
      and dullard junk-prophecy

I've been to Omaha, bro.
  It'll never be the our nations capitol
    not even nuclear devastation
      will make the place more palatable
      The cockroaches are lined up
        En masse for a greyhound bus

A corvette, bro?
  Are you kidding me
    It's a rust trap
    A death knell.
      You must be joshing
        I'm up to my neck in your bullshit
        And all I can hear is the sloshing

John Titor,
  You're living in your momma's basement, bro
    In Garland, Texas surrounded by lotion
      You send your fantasy over

An electronic ocean hoping
Other fat nerds believe you.

Forgive me, bro,
  if I just dismiss you.

OUT ON THE EDGE ...

My life is more than just a redundant collection
    of moves witnessed and forgotten.
My life is not just another version
    of Dr. Zhivago on a widescreen, muted.
My life is not just a poorly executed chess game
    where all the pawns have been sacrificed
    all the rooks smoke crack on the corner
    all the knights are jockeying oblique positions
    Just to get next to some ethnic queen

And I'm stuck moving in slow motion,
Out on the edge
In enemy territory
Moving Slowly
One thought at a time

They say that
Every game of chess
    is often ruled by its opening
Every move has a consequence
Every advance forces a fallback
Every mistake costs life

And every prize takes sacrifice
That's the nature of it

VERY LOW SODIUM ...

Wake up, Slave
   Didn't you realize,
      That the deeper you are into hell,
         The nicer it is?
         The larger the open spaces
         The greener the lawn
         The bluer the sky
         The looser the coin

Wake up, Slave
   Don't you realize,
The reason the Muzak is so deafening,
   Everywhere you go?
         Target
         Wal-Mart
         Banana Republic
         Olive Garden
         The Mall
It's camouflage
   For the status-quo
You should be rebelling by now
   But your not

Wake up, Slave
   Don't you see,
What's going on around you?
   It doesn't bother you
That most of you are dying
         From something unknown
         And incurable
         That most of your children have mutated
         Most of your children have autism
         Most of your children are retarded

Wake up, Slave
Don't you understand?
That the nicer it is
The more it's going to hurt

8

When the trap springs shut on you
You wake up and find your foot gone
And the door closed
The lights off and utter silence
The air will smell like rotting bodies
and chemicals
And you aren't able to move

Like I told you, Slave,
  The nicer it is
    The deeper in hell you truly are
Maybe you should wake up
  And respond
Maybe I should just let the
  Hordes of pedophiles that roam free
    Take you and rape you
Maybe I should just let your government
  Find you guilty and imprison you

You're not innocent anymore
  So stop crying.

'You're all a bunch of fucking slaves!"
- James Douglas Morrison

WHEN I SEE YOUR FACE ... I'M SLEEPING

Somewhere
In the back of your female brain
          When you think of me
          When you say my name
          When you see my face

You move into fields
Of post-traumatic stress
And
          It's Def-Con One
          It's Systems Alert
          It's Spyware detected
          It's a Foreign Intrusion

It's all the things you wish
          You hadn't remembered
And probably all the things you wish
          You could've completely deleted

Somewhere
In the back of your female brain
You still suspect me
You're still expecting me
          Thinking I'm nearby
          In hiding

To you
I'm just a stalker
To you
I'm just an object
Standing in your way
          Like a toll-gate
          That's too expensive
          Like a CIA contract
          That keeps you from living
          That keeps you in hiding
          Like a novel
          That keeps repeating
          That keeps reminding

10

You think you see me
        Behind every door
You think you hear me
        Behind every questionable call

I wish I'd never met you at times
        Because I wonder
            Just where I might be now

I wish I'd never heard your voice
        Because I'd sleep at nights
            In peace and be free now

Handfuls of years dissolve away
Tears into the ocean ~ but nothing's changed

I'm not your friend now
I'm not your lover now
I'm not your neighbor now
Still your adversary now
But I'm not your stalker now
I'm not your father now
I'm not your past now
And laughingly
I'm not your future

The way it is
I'm nothing now

So …
        Bury the hatchet – it's over
        Bury the past – it'll just slow you

When I see your face
I'm sleeping and
When I hear your voice
I'm still listening …

YOU SAID: GO TO HELL ...

I'm wasting my breath on you
But I care too much
Not to mention

I'm wasting my time with you
But I'm too invested now
To release you

I'm dying inside with you
But I sit by idly, nightly
Unable to tell you

I'm rotting in this king size bed beside you
But my sexual knee-jerk reactions
Won't let me pull out of you

My soul will burn in hell with you
But I'm just too bitter, darling
To point out the landscape that's quickly passing
In front of you

VOX INTERRUPTUS ...

The post menopausal siren
Bleating away beside me
A train wreck in waiting
Oblivious to the chemical estrogen
That's overwhelming you
When you're alone with your crack-pipe body
You're dreaming of cutting your wrists
Polishing that shot-gun shell
Ready to imbibe
Taking your clit out for a brisk
You're the bane of the populous masses
Cackling away
A dried up hag
Blank stare
Hollow eyes
Mad at the flesh
On your chest
That you value
That's now thin, flat
Drooping sadly
You can't ignore
The inevitable ...
   Flapjack sag

FORGOTTEN GULF ...

I sat awake
In a chemical haze
Drinking cigarettes till 2 am
We traversed the green skyline at night
Watching the show through NVG's
The radio call came through from the General's Mess
We sent them Artillery
Air mail express
My enlisted companions guffawed real slow
The night sky thundered like electric buffalo

These shells do not sound like the ocean

Moments later the crippling blast shook us
Then the warm sub-nuclear waves of decision
Passed through us
Children removed from within us

What I'm telling you
Is classified: 'confidential'
Military Secrets
That I only think about
Drinking cigarettes
In a chemical haze at 2 am

Thank you for choosing McDonald's
For any comments or concerns
contact our Store Manager

7950 FOOTHILL BLVD
SUNLAND, CA 91040

THANK YOU

MCDONALDS **S#1**   TEL# (818)352-7456
39 KS#01   JUL 30'06(Sun)08:57
STORE# 3331

Order #139   EAT IN

1 SAU EGG MCMUFFIN ML	2.40
1 SM COFFEE	1.29
SUB TOTAL	3.69
EAT IN TAX	0.30
CASH TENDERED	20.00
CHANGE	16.01

Thank you for choosing Planet Earth
For any comments or concerns
contact your Fellow Man

7950 FOOTHILL BLVD
SUNLAND, CA 91040

WE'RE LAUGHING AT YOU

REALITY   **S#1**   TEL# (818)974-0805

STORE# 666   JUL 30'06(Sun)08:57

Order #YOU   DYING

1 Esophageal Cancer   Years of Pain
1 Dozen Stomach Ulcers   Suffering

SUB TOTAL   DEATH
EAT IN TAX   HAPPINESS

CASH TENDERED   LIFE
CHANGE   YOU BETTER

16

K416 (BLACK)

I want to tell you about a few things –
Lately gone 'black'
In our science community
Super Black projects that receive easy funding
Whilst your local kindergarten does not

    Atom Smashers are getting ready
    LHC at CERN comes on line tomorrow
    Tiny black holes will be appearing
    Probably the size of a child's iris
    Slowly taking us all inside

Kirtland Air Force Base
Albuquerque
    Sandia labs Eggheads are plotting
    Tinker toy size nano-machines
    Replicating themselves
    Ad-infinitesimal
    Creating the dreaded soup of grey goo
    That will cover the Earth entirely
    In just a mere two days

I want to tell you about a few things –
Lately gone 'black'
In our science community
Super Black projects that receive easy funding
Whilst your local kindergarten does not

    Army War College documents
    Can step-by-step you into
    Creating like some Nuevo-God
    A low-grade, hasty equivalent
    Of a billion dollar EMP Weapon
    With your neighbors cheap microwave
    I say 'neighbor's' because
    I need to inform you that
    A microwave conductor
      Was – NEVER –

Meant for household use
And I don't have one
At least not in my kitchen
I keep it in the garage, surgically altered
Unused with a mini-generator

And while we're lounging kitchen-side
Keep cooking on Teflon
And smiling and chewing politely
Remarking
'How easy it is to clean my pans'
While not realizing
Why Autism has skyrocketed
Since 1950
While you close your eyes and struggle to not see a
connection
It was meant to deter bullets on the battlefield
Not heat up to 200
and prepare your meals upon

What I'm telling you can only be voxed
In this format -
Canterbury tales et poetics
Else I'd be shot
Taken from my comfortable home
Sans microwave
And not heard from again

I want to tell you about a few things –
Lately gone 'black'
In our science community
Super Black projects that receive easy funding
Whilst your local kindergarten does not

WATCHING FROM MY TABLE AT BREAKFAST ...

Commuters
  Travelers
    Family-men
Traversing this cold Los Angeles morning
  Speeding the streets
    Pressing down on the pedal hard
      Trying to avoid the rain, the fog, real-life
Panicking over an immaculate drive
The luxury car that might just meet wet weather
  Runs the Redlight
    Talking on a Bluetooth
      Snuffs out the Black man
      Rolls hard
        Across the smooth grey hood
White decision decides to
Push on – unseen
Finishes off the brown mud – cold coffee
Doesn't give a dry shite about
  A Yellow light
    Only the Green cost of what
      Could've been
Didn't care to wear Orange
A Department of Corrections jumpsuit

Clean getaway once more
The guilt is washed away
Clear

PLEASE, SOMEONE ANSWER ME ...

Why do I believe in brotherhood
   When I am surrounded by adversaries?

Why do I believe in brotherhood
   When I'm taking the sniper's blast
      Directly to the face
        From across the fetid cesspool of my friends?

Why do I believe in brotherhood
   In a city like Los Angeles
      That sells souls as if they were
        Cheap plastic bags that you might put your bullshit in?

Why do I believe in brotherhood
   In a country like the United States
      When gang-bangers are taking money bets
      to see who'll gut me first?

Why do I believe in brotherhood
   In a world such as this
      That sees only my credit report
      My social security number
      My wallet
      But not my face ?

In this life
   As it sours in front of me
   And I age and become obsolete ...

Why do I believe in brotherhood?

MY WEINER DOG ...

Blistering hot
The Burbank sun is baking the slaves
   out for their sick gravy lunches
Studio executives who dress
   like all their clothes came from
   Wal-Mart or their filthy old uncle
   who smelled of sour milk and
   never washed his clothes

My Wiener Dog wants to kill these people
Almost as badly as I do
She stares ... fixated and intense
Watching the day-time soap trolls passing on the sidewalk
If she could rip their face off
   and bury them in a shallow grave
She'd feel actualized
She'd smile, bark and patrol the windows

I watch the madness unfold everyday
   from the comfort and breadth of my large white sofa
   In my Californian two-bedroom
   plastic and plaster labyrinth
     My wooden wind chime
      Dangling
       Like a dried corpse
        Drying in the sun
          Blowing in the crisp, hot winter wind
          Of this eighty degree world
          With clear skies
          And Screaming Police sirens
          In the distance
          looking long and wide
          for an old girlfriend

My Wiener Dog would chew on strychnine and slurp whiskey
  If I asked her to

We find strange ways to cope
  We find strange ways to live
    We find strange ways to breed
      In this nightmarish and dark landscape of a city
We find different ways of getting through
  This bone-bleached world
              Of hustlers,
              travelers
              and salesmen
        Selling the world,
              Pimping radiation,
              Hustling a bone bleach

All of you whores
  reading this now
    consuming the planet
      like there's a fucking back-up

My Wiener Dog
  will fucking
    end
      all of you

JOHN WAYNE ...

This is me. Is that you?
I heard you're in Hell now
How's the food?
Did they set you up with a ranch and a hay barn?
Do you spend time riding charred souls
    into the lake of fire?

I saw your reflection in plate glass
    While walking the strip in downtown Palm Springs
    It was 120 degrees out and rising
But you were shivering and looking for an open flame
Hoping to keep warm

I was told:
    They didn't care too much for Hondo down there either ...
    That they no longer call you 'The Duke' ...
    That you've shacked up with an Englishman ...
    That you love to watch porno in the afternoons ...
    And that on Sundays you go to church
    And play horseshoes with Heinrich Himmler

I was told all the flesh on your corpulent frame melted
And you now appear
As black
As a burnt marshmallow
      Imagine the irony
      Imagine your friends

Palm Springs is the only place on Earth
That's close enough to Hell where
Sometimes you cross over
      You looked fine to me
      But maybe it was just a disguise
      Maybe it was my mind

You were trying to tell me that
Someone I knew was sorry

That they wanted to apologize

You were mumbling and coughing over my shoulder
Like you had pneumonia and it was winter
I stopped and watched you in the reflection
Of the Starbucks window-glass
People inside thought I'd lost my mind
They thought I was talking to myself
They couldn't see you, or probably didn't want to ...
That's okay, I don't blame them

Tell the son of a bitch I don't want an apology
Lottery numbers are better proof that he feels my pain
I doubt he'd comply
He wouldn't do anything that would make his soul burn hotter
Especially not for me

I'm getting awful tired of running into you like this ...
Out on the street, and on my way to dinner
I can only speak in code so much before I'm completely bored
People might begin to talk
I was never a fan, nor did I enjoy your movies
You probably would've blacklisted me as well
    Had I known you then

I read a book about you in High School
It said you were a jackass to a lot of people
Including your family
I guess you got what you deserved
You were made moot from unseen fall-out
It completed you
It absorbed you
The nuclear winter of your own private Utah

They ripped your chest in half
When they harvested your soul
Your limbs dangled from the side board
And your expression wilted
Did you taste the juice
    When they embalmed you?

Did you feel the floor drop out
   When they convicted you?

Tell me …
John Wayne
This is me
Is that you?

PAUL WELLER & GOD ...

When the Style Council
    become the soundtrack
        for Starbucks consumers
            at six am
                I want out ...

When the only thing to watch
    On every goddamned channel
        Is Anna Nicole Smith
            Sean Hannity and MASH
                I want out ...

When all the overhead Muzak
    Is raping Stevie Winwood
        Aping The Police
            Van Morrison or
                Bruce Hornsby and the Range
                    I want out ...

When the country is struggling
    To fit neatly and quietly
        Into the status quo
            For selfish reasons of their own
                I want out ...

When the only person I care about
    Is myself and yet I don't
        Have a clue as to
            Who I am
                I want out ...

When the snow caps are finished
    The polar bears are a myth and dusted
        When the Dolphins declare:
            So long, and thanks for all the fish
                I'll be out.

CONTROL ALTERNATE DELETE ...

Hideously deformed
Gnarled faces of aged Robots
Peer and blink into the
Blank air – unmated

Seven minutes
Twenty six seconds
Until your designated lunch break ends

I feel like an intruder
Mingling among you
Hoping to find your off switch
Unplug you
Power down

If I could reprogram you
Upload new subroutines
Delete your old task log
Leave your software open-ended
    Make you a target
    Within the mainframe
Run Spyware
Put your world into quarantine
Make you witness a reboot
Reformat

WHAT A FOOL BELIEVES, HE SEES ...

Every time you speak
"What a fool believes"
Is playing in my back brain

You have no idea
Of the soundtracks
That I have on standby
    As your loose jaw
    Breaks wind
    And cackles

Michael McDonald
Is screaming
It's an unintentional consequence
Of your dullard upbringing
    Too many drugs
    Too much booze
    Not enough down time
    You're harboring a stooge

Grinding away in nighttime traffic
You'll become a SIG alert
    Transmitted over the news
Caught on evening freeway
As the sun fades
    Listening to a white man's blues

WINSLOW HOMER IN THE BACKGROUND ...

All my friends are in pain
I can see it burned deep
The cattle brands
On their cold grey faces
Francis Bacon paintings of the street

People are so much younger
Then I remember them
Vibrant
Searching but still lost
In a world full of bastards
Drifting to their own advice
Quiet minds
Sifted and strained
Through some
Personal electronic device

Their dreams drain me and draw me out
Conversations like club-music
Winslow Homer in the background
I can only feel compassion
I can only believe
One day you'll grow up
And then maybe you'll see

NOTHING IS WORTH GETTING LOST OVER ...

Unless of course ...
You're completely fucking lost ...
It's pitch black ...
And you're not wearing any shoes ...
You didn't bring the condoms ...
You didn't bring your wallet ...
Your bus pass or your cell phone.

Some days our pain is intentional ...

Some days our depression
is just the 'JACKPOT'
of our own self-indulgence.

Sometimes it's better
to enjoy it
before it fades away
and the sun comes out ...
and your friends call ...
and your man brings you flowers ...
and your woman shows up light brown
and in pink cotton pannies ...

Nothing is worth getting lost over
Not even love

THE LIGHT OF MANKIND ...

When the lights go out on mankind
The dark will be turned on

It will rise up quick
Surround us
The past will not just come back to haunt us
But lay
Absolute
Fucking
Siege to us

Everything you know
Everything you ever held dear
Will evaporate in moments
Your world will vanish
like the birds after an A-bomb

It will be worse
Than any vision
    that:
    John Carpenter
    George Romero
    or Adolf Hitler
Could've ever imagined

It will be reality
And it will be unceasing

I've seen it
I've been there
I did not survive
But I tried.

GAS AND EUTHANASIA ...

Los Angeles smells like
Mexican ladies using laundry soap
Homeless men sifting through the county landfill
White women in well-lit homes rubbing their naked loins in
lavender.

Los Angeles feels like
It's about to rain but holds out on you indef
A continual turf-war for Black Gorilla Family and 18th Street
An island of fools, trapped inside an outdoor prison unable to
leave
A financial vice-grip around your throat, your life, your belief
in god

Los Angeles continues like
You don't mind and you don't matter
City Politicians are only in it for themselves
Local Law Enforcement would rather shoot you first and
forget to ask questions later.

Los Angeles is divided like
Inmates are in prison
First white, then brown, then black, then yellow
Those with money and those with money
The old waiting to die and the young waiting to be raped

Los Angeles smells like
A graveyard
Smog during rush-hour traffic
Tears down a mother's cheek
A cage at the pound that once held a frightened dog

Los Angeles smells like gas and euthanasia.

IN A MOMENT ...

If I said I saw it coming
You wouldn't believe me

If I told you it was closer
To any of us
Then you could imagine
You'd laugh
Shrug
Scratch your head
Turn on the TV
Get in the car
And go to Costco

You probably already feel it
Even without me
You can sense it closing
Even without this

It's going to happen

ATTENTION ...

All you broke dicks, street queens,
gambolers, hustlers
And shit-pimps

You'll struggle, whine and bleed
Trying to find some way to get through the gate
Hoping to penetrate pop culture
With your fake names, fake breasts and your dull personality

You're a bunch of old world communists
Struggling for control
   Another player on team slacker
   Looking to take over
   And fuck it all up
   Just like the rest of them

24 MONTHS ...

The cities that
  Cover the earth
  Blinking off and on
  As the days pass
    Seen from space
    Could be construed
      As one giant
      Scream
      In Morse code

Calling out
Across the infinite
For help
Maybe a little direction
Maybe some guidance
    But you know that
    No one's coming

There'll be no answers
    At least not of the kind
    That you're going to find
    Pleasing
At least not of the kind
That's going to end well
I don't think you know just
How close
To the end of the timer
We are

I don't think you realize
That things are about to change permanently
You're going to have to be more than you are
You're going to have to reach down inside yourself
Because I assure you
    It might
    Make all
    The difference

EVERYONE'S ALWAYS BAREFOOT ...

I'm watching cartoons at three am
Robots rule the earth
Terrorizing civilians
Bulldozing progress like
The last thousand years
Was just a wank

Ape-men run screaming
Under continuous variances
Of death rays, missile arrays, cat hands
And god knows what

But did you notice
Everyone's always barefoot
And wearing apocalypse garb
And hungry

The psychological consciousness
Of all of us
Already was dialed in
Already in understanding of
The future in front of us

The mechanism of modern man
The artistic bible of our fate
Represented at
24 frames per second

SWITCH ...

Your fate is enclosing around you
Your last moments are just around the corner
The wagons are circled
The bow strings are pulled
And taught

The last few days of
    The morning news
    Calm moments over coffee
    Long walks with the dog
    In the dead of night
        Are over

Could the last one to die
    Just please
        Turn out the lights

MY WEAKNESS ...

You fuckers know my weakness
I was reading your poetry
About the Ipswich Strangler
When you launched it
I was deep in thought
When you said it
I was down the rabbit hole
And sinking when you
Brought it

Soft and warm
Easy to cup
Put my hands on
Labor over
Get lost in
   Slip
      down
         the rabbit-hole
          forever over

Should I add my cream?
Aren't you sweet enough?
I'd drive hours for the best of you
I'd slay myself in my worst moments
Just to have you
Can't you see I'm addicted?
Can't you see I'm inflicted?

Maybe Jarvis Cocker could save me?
Maybe taking a long bath could displace it?
Maybe the sick rush of adrenaline would push me?
Just to give in and destroy you

You fuckers know my weakness
I was reading your poetry
About the Ipswich Strangler
When you launched it

INSTRUCTION SET .01 ...

When it begins
    You're going to have to move quick
The problem is
    You'll probably be sleeping
Your response time will be critical
    The first thirty minutes
    Will be everything
    It will not be a test

If you own a motorcycle
    Don't take it
You'll be tempted to
    Because of the economy of fuel
But don't do it
Being exposed
    Will be a death sentence
Others will think like you did
They'll be desperate
    You'll end up getting shot
    Crashing
    Left bleeding beside the road
    With your dead loved one
    Somewhere just behind you

Head North, head for higher ground
    Get out of town
Don't take the obvious routes
    Stay off the freeways
    For Christ's sakes
    Don't go downtown
    You're not Charlton Heston

Only grab a gun if you're absolutely sure
    You can use it
A ball bat is far more effective
A Machete is step two
Firearms are too noisy

Extra Ammo is too heavy
And bullets will become more scarce
   With every passing day

Don't get caught up looting
   Unnecessary Crap
   Will only weigh you down

Everything will happen quickly
   If you don't have a gas mask
   Make one
Wrap your head with a wet cloth
Water is preferable over gasoline

       This might sound insane
         But look –
         For Winona Ryder

       This might sound insane
         But look –
         For Winona Ryder

       This might sound insane
         But look up high
         For Winona Ryder

INSTRUCTION SET .02 ...

You might be told to stay home
    Relax
    Don't Panic

Remember what I told you
    It's a stall
    To maintain order
You'll need to get free of the city
    Hopefully
    Before everybody else does

The TV will go to static
Your Cell phone wont have signal
And the power grid will blacken
People's fear is going to explode
    And the only real fuel source
    Will be your will to live

Certain things will begin
Below the surface
    Unsuspected
It will be more than
    Rat Poison in dog food
    A Pollen Coating that's described
    As a 'Yellow Sheen'
    Or another outbreak
    Of hoof-in-mouth

It will begin on a Tuesday
    And by Friday
    If you're still at home
I'll feel for you

Large groups of well-armed black men
Will band together in gangs
    And try to seize control of
    Property, weapons and women

41

Scattered bands of middle-aged
Murderous white-men
    Will be quietly scavenging the perimeter
    In fixed desperation

Families will board themselves together
    In cul-de-sac communities
    And then savagely turn on each other
Once they're
Out of food
Out of water
Out of hope
Out of choices

Everyone you meet
    Will evaluate you
    Like a product
    Assess you
    Kill you
    And collect your
    Supplies

You may not want to hear this
    You probably don't
        Want to know
You may not make it out
    With your loved ones
     And sadly
You may not make it out at all

        This might sound insane
          But look –
          For Winona Ryder

        This might sound insane
          But look –
          For Winona Ryder

        This might sound insane
          But look up high
          For Winona Ryder

I BELIEVE I HAVE AN ANSWER ...

What use is poetry?
The words assaulted my inner ear with
Dumbed-down public-school reverence
Lacking real sincerity
Absent of real internal ingenuity

> I felt against the wall
> I was on the Offensive

Poetry is not a means to an end
I answered
It's not a war to be waged
And won by the time we get here
It's not a service pistol
Full of brass rounds
That I'll use against you
The next time we square off

It's more like a dull, rusted knife
Found abandoned
In a muddy creek
Where I'll spend the next fifteen years
Slowly trying to perfect it
Using a piece of rotted wood
Or the decaying carcass of some
Unidentifiable mammal
So that one day
It will be sharper than surgical steel
Which will pierce you
And rip out your insides
Trying to exorcise you
Of pretense
And dullard communication

It's everything you're trying to understand
That your television can't teach you
Can't show you
Cannot deliver

It's the message you've been lacking
The internal order that you were waiting for
It's the left turn you'll have to one day face

It's a long time out
But not now

INDEX ...

Born in Pennsylvania in 1971 and raised in England and various parts of Alaska. Attended school at the University of Alaska, Anchorage and the University of Los Angeles, California.

Steffan has lived in many places across the globe with a purpose bent on never being a tourist in his own home, town or country. Once a resident of Alaska, the Mayor of Nome, John Handelin, asked him to 'leave and never return', due to a minor misunderstanding.

He has been oft-quoted as being an alien in all environments and unable to find his true home. He is disliked by most, but loved enough. He has an undying love of physics, literature and Caravaggio.

www.ingramcontent.com/pod-product-compliance
Lightning Source LLC
Chambersburg PA
CBHW021226020426
42331CB00003B/491